Croatia Travel Guide

Everything You Need to Know Before Trip to Croatia

By
Roger P. k. Guide

CROATIA
TRAVEL GUIDE

Everything You Need To Know Before Trip To Croatia

Roger P.k. Guide

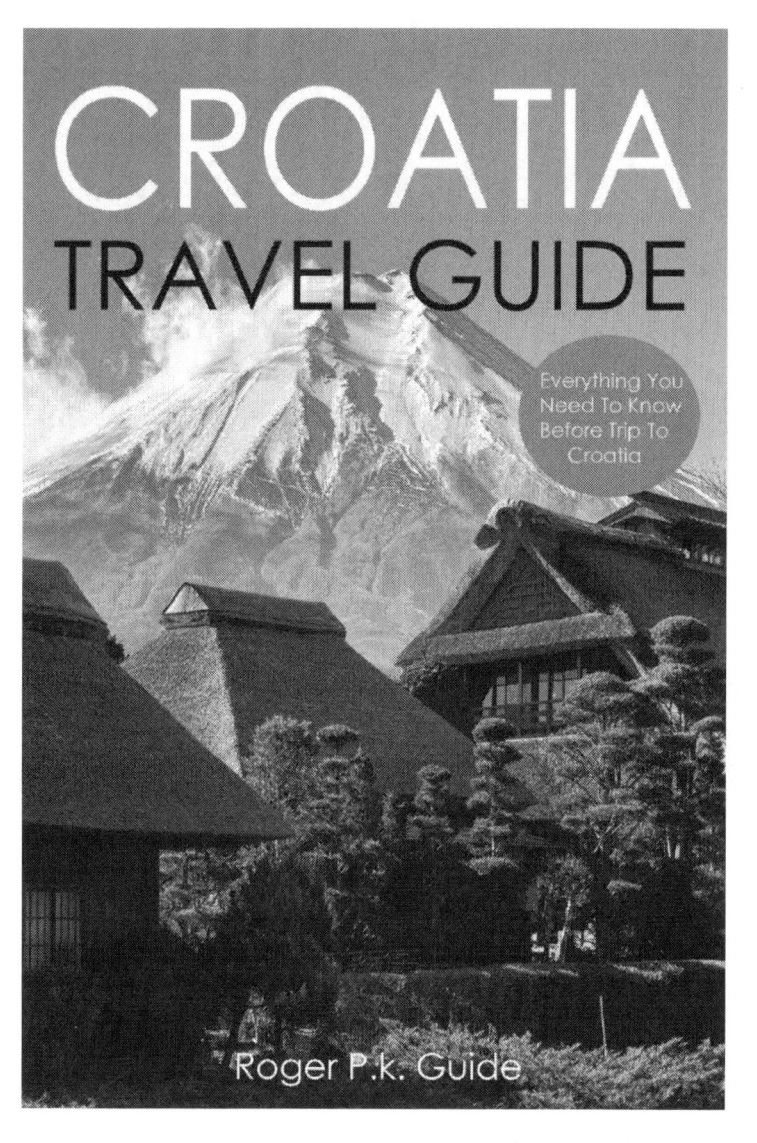

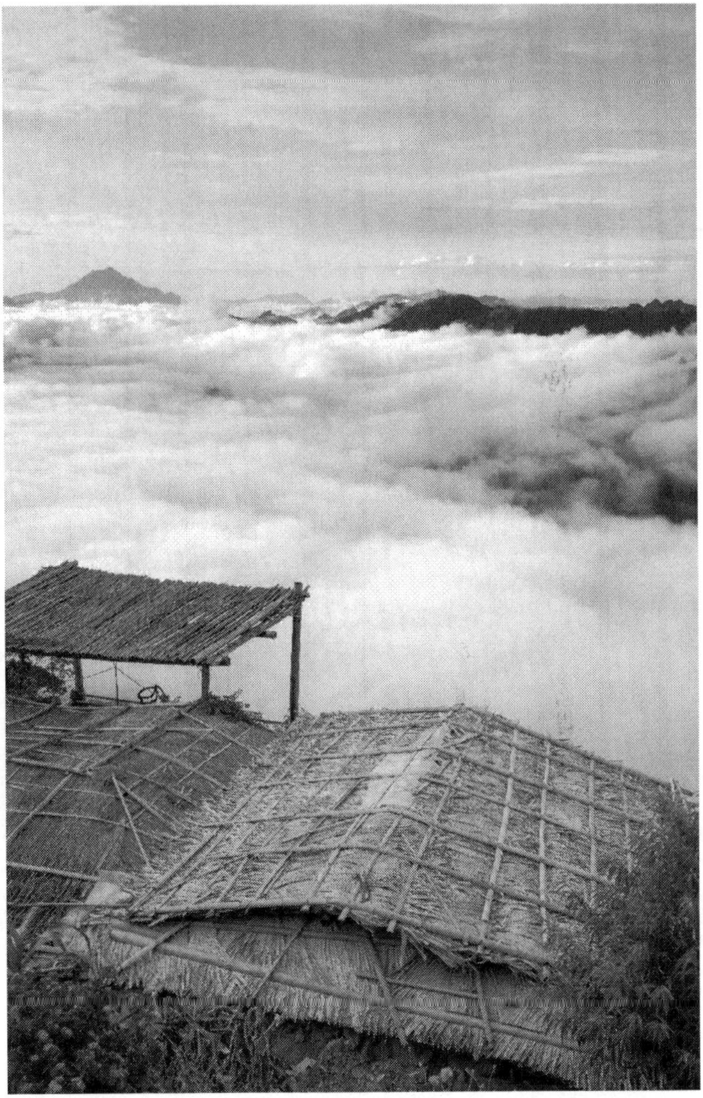

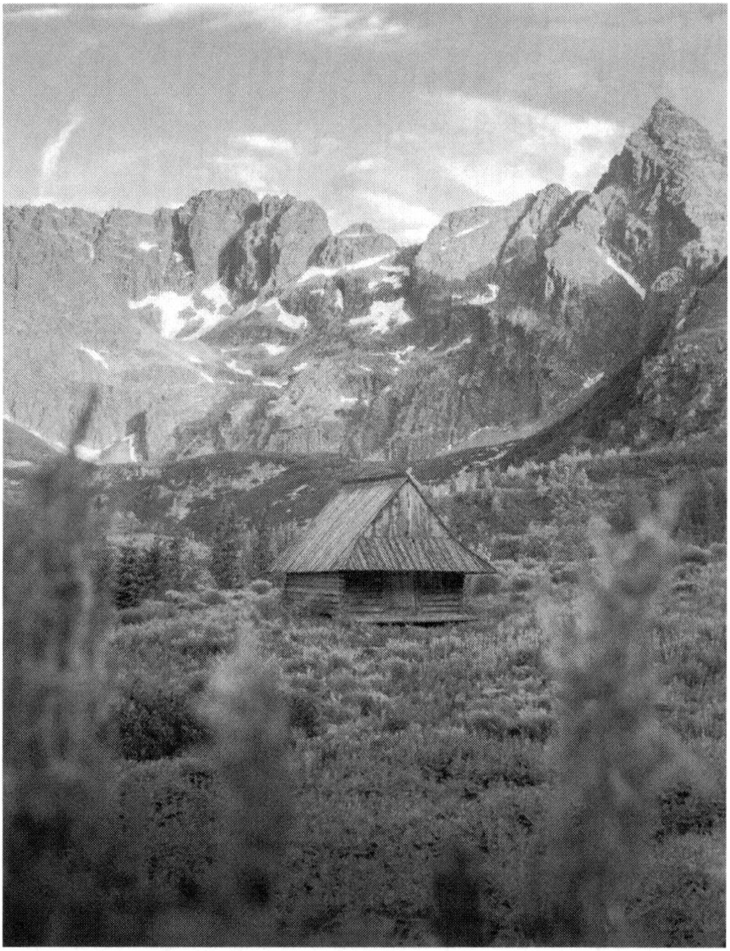

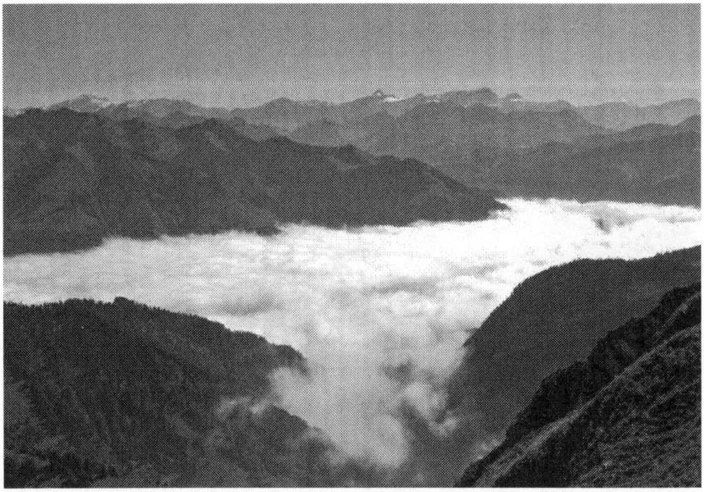

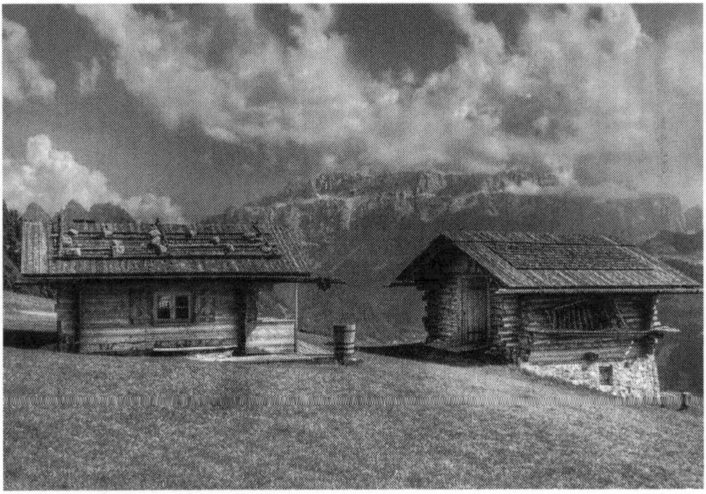

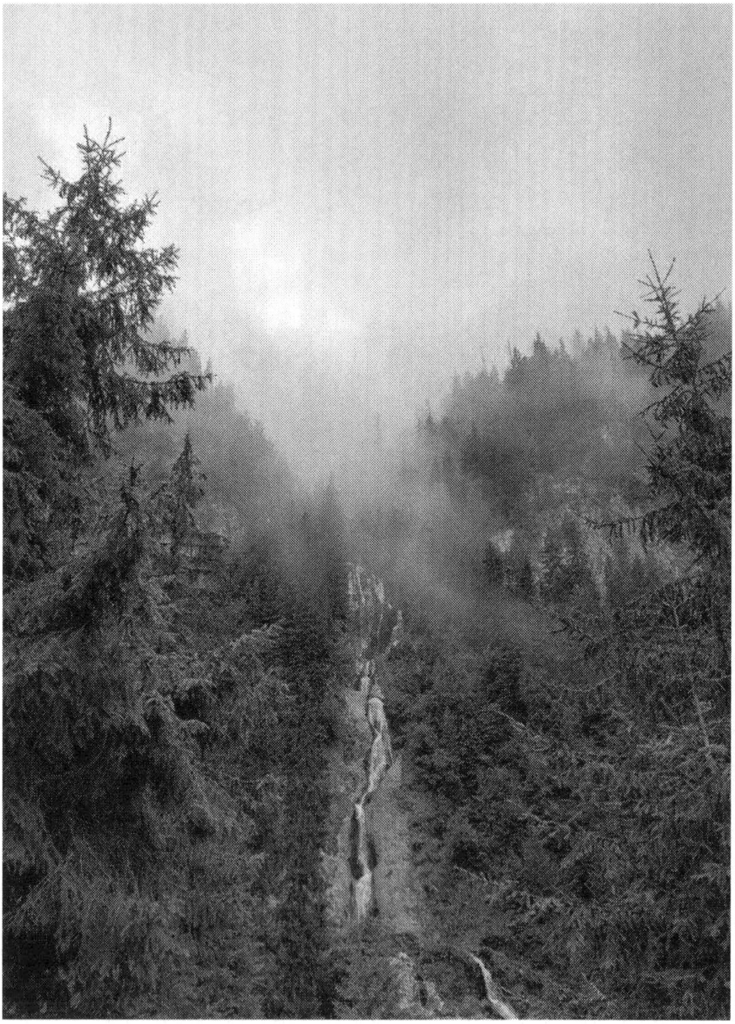

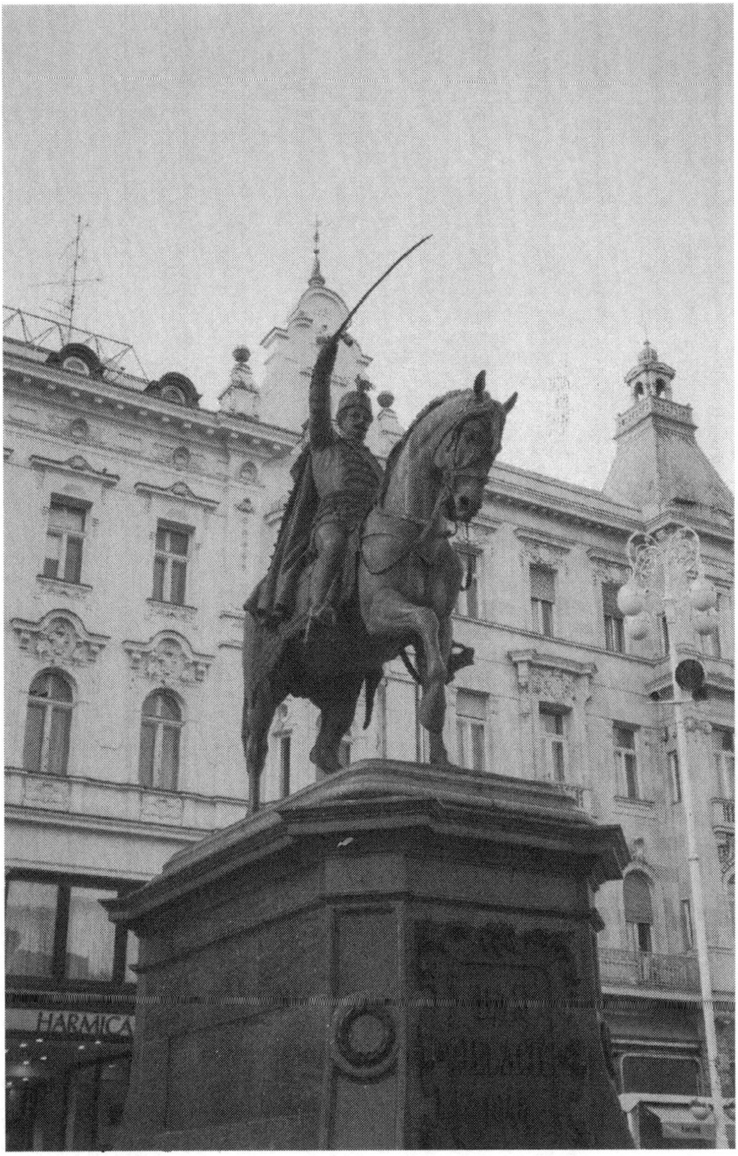
HARMICA

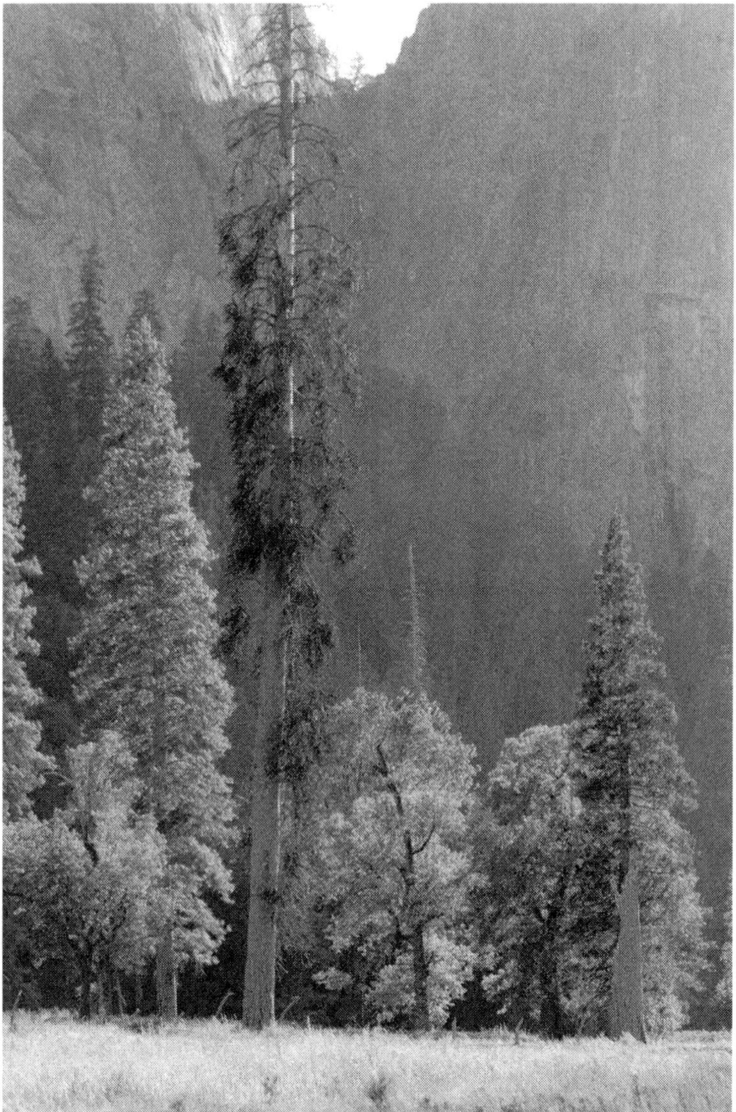

Table of Content

Introduction 14

Chapter 1: Getting to Know Croatia 21
Croatia at a Glance: Geographical Overview 22
Croatia's Rich History and Cultural Heritage 22
Climate and Best Time to Visit 23
Festivals and Events in Croatia 24

Chapter 2: Essential Travel Planning 27
Visa Requirements and Travel Documents 28
Currency, Banking, and Exchange Rates 29
Transportation Options: Getting Around Croatia 30
Accommodation Choices: From Budget to Luxury 31

Chapter 3: Top Destinations in Croatia 34
Dubrovnik: The Pearl of the Adriatic 35
Split: Ancient City with Modern Vibes 36
Zagreb: The Vibrant Capital 37
Plitvice Lakes National Park: Nature's Masterpiece 38
Old Town: UNESCO World Heritage Site 39
City Walls and Fortresses 40
Lokrum Island and Nearby Attractions 41
Diocletian's Palace: A Roman Marvel 41
Marjan Hill and Park 42

Nearby Islands: Hvar, Brac, and Vis 43
Upper Town (Gornji Grad) and Lower Town (Donji Grad)
.... 43
St. Mark's Church and Zagreb Cathedral 44
Museums, Galleries, and Cultural Hotspots 44
Plitvice Lakes National Park: Nature's Masterpiece 45
The Stunning Cascade of Lakes and Waterfalls 46
Hiking and Exploring the Park 46
Tips for a Memorable Visit 47

Chapter 4: Exploring the Adriatic Coast 49
Istria: The Tuscany of Croatia 50
Pula and its Roman Heritage 55
Rovinj: A Charming Seaside Town 55
Wine and Gastronomy in Istria 56
The Dalmatian Islands: A Sailing Paradise 56
Hvar: Lavender Fields and Nightlife 61
Vis: Tranquility and Authentic Mediterranean Experience
.... 62
Korcula: Marco Polo's Birthplace 62
Zadar and Sibenik: Lesser-Known Gems 63
Zadar: Sea Organ and Sun Salutation 67
Sibenik: Medieval Architecture and Krka National Park. 68
Off-the-Beaten-Path Experiences 69

Chapter 5: Adventure and Outdoor Activities 71
Kayaking and Sailing the Adriatic Sea 72
Hiking and Trekking in Croatia's National Parks 73
Scuba Diving and Snorkeling in Crystal Clear Waters 74

Cycling Routes and Bike Tours 75
Chapter 6: Croatian Cuisine and Wine 77
Traditional Dishes and Culinary Delights 78
Wine Regions and Tastings 79
Local Food Experiences and Cooking Classes 80

Chapter 7: Practical Tips and Cultural Etiquette 82
Useful Croatian Phrases and Language Tips 83
Safety and Emergency Contacts 84
Local Customs and Etiquette 85

Chapter 8: Resources and Further Reading 87
Recommended Books and Travel Guides 88
Online Resources and Websites 89
Acknowledgments and Credits 90

Conclusion 92
Recap of Croatia's Highlights 92
Final Tips and Recommendations 93
Inspiring Readers to Plan Their Croatian Adventure 94

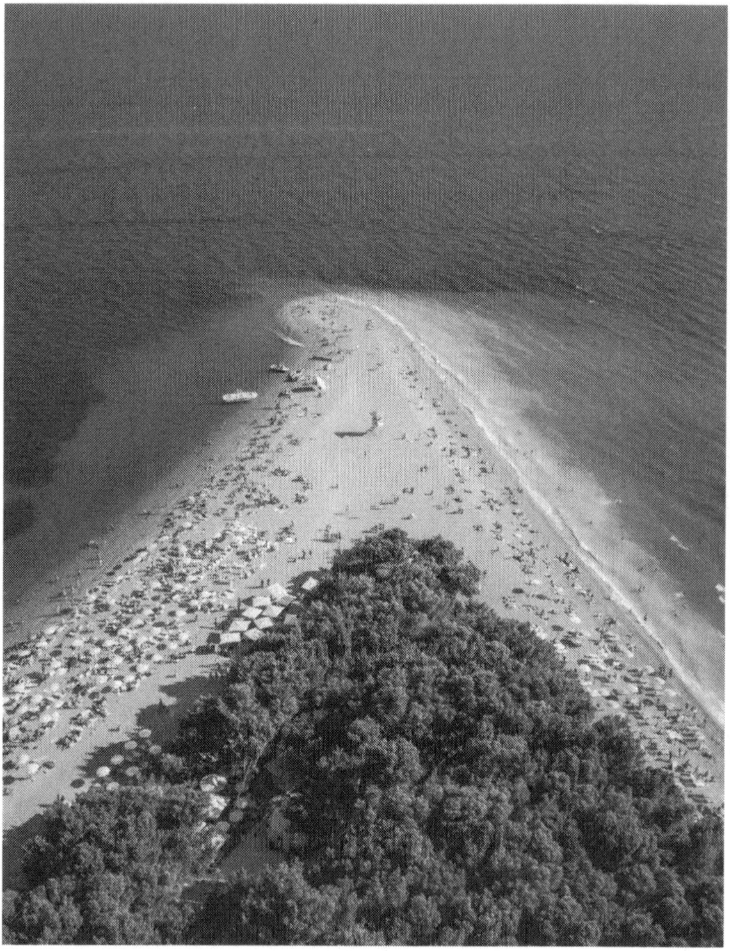

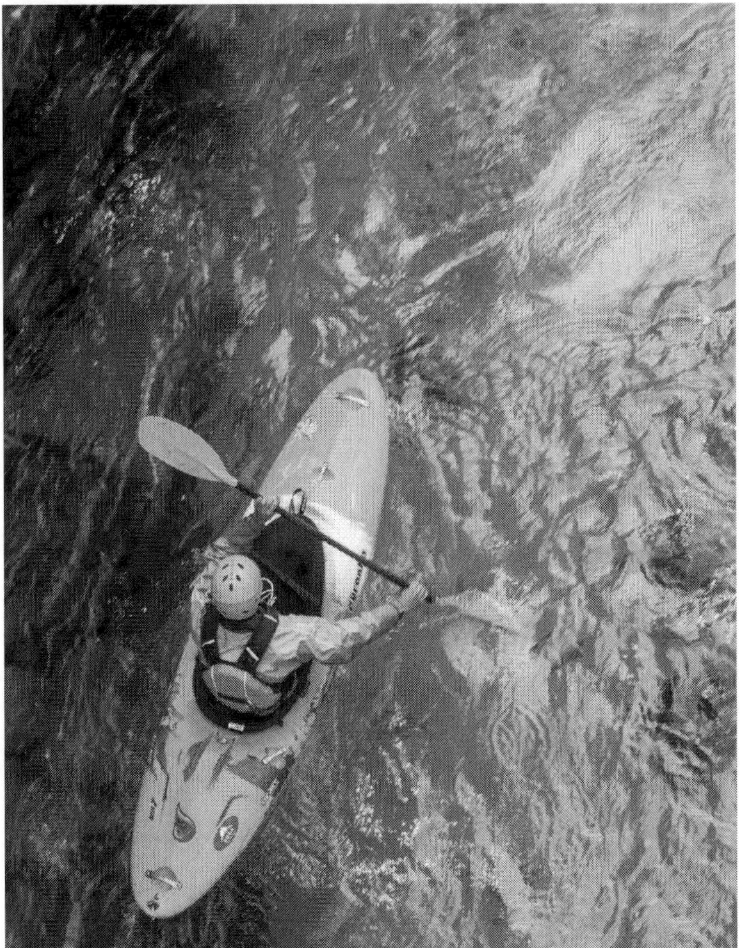

Introduction

Hello, and welcome to Croatia! Here you'll find travel guides that will help you discover the best of the Land of a Thousand Islands.

You have arrived in Croatia, sometimes known as the Land of a Thousand Islands.

Get ready to go on an enthralling adventure down the sun-kissed Adriatic coast as we encourage you to see Croatia, the stunning country of a thousand islands, and prepare to do it in style by visiting us in Croatia. The tourist experience that can be had in Croatia is genuinely unparalleled due to the country's untouched beaches, centuries-old cities, and breathtaking natural scenery. This Mediterranean jewel has the promise of magic around every corner, from the world-famous city walls of Dubrovnik to the lively alleys of Zagreb. Get ready to completely submerge yourself in the lively culture of Croatia, indulge in the delectable food, and make memories that will stick with you for the rest of your life.

The Reasons Why Croatia Is Such an Amazing Tourist Destination

Numerous factors contribute to the fact that Croatia is such a great location for vacationers to visit. Ancient ruins that have been meticulously preserved, museums that captivate visitors, and festivals that honor the past all attest to the city's wealth in historical and cultural legacy. Visitors are left in wonder by the country's breathtakingly diverse landscapes, which range from the awe-inspiring Plitvice Lakes National Park to the Adriatic Sea, which is known for its turquoise seas. The warm friendliness and genuine charm of Croatia, together with the country's dynamic cities and picture-perfect islands, combine to make for a once-in-a-lifetime experience that wins over the affections of tourists from all walks of life.

The eBook's Aims and Organizational Framework

This e-book was written with the intention of becoming your most reliable travel companion while you explore the marvels of Croatia. We have painstakingly developed a detailed guide that will assist you in getting the most out of your vacation by providing you with helpful insights, actionable advice, and suggestions from local experts.

This eBook features a structure that is straightforward and simple to use, and it is broken up into chapters that focus on different parts of your trip. Following a brief introduction to the geography, history, and climate of Croatia, we will walk you through the fundamentals of trip preparation, including the procedures for obtaining a visa, the different modes of transportation, and the many lodging possibilities. Our handpicked collection of top locations, which includes Dubrovnik, Split, Zagreb, and Plitvice Lakes National Park, will emphasize the most important aspects of each area and provide you with the opportunity to thoroughly immerse yourself in the special allure of each one.

However, it is not the end of the exciting journey. We are going to take you on an exciting journey down the Adriatic Coast, beginning in the picture-perfect area of Istrian and continuing on to the gorgeous islands of Dalmatia. A chapter has been devoted to outdoor sports such as kayaking, hiking, scuba diving, and cycling so that you may enjoy a first-hand experience of the natural beauties that Croatia has to offer. If you are an adventurous soul, this chapter is for you.

And what could be a more enjoyable way to learn about the culture of Croatia than to do it via its mouthwatering cuisine and wines that are recognized all over the world? You will be introduced to traditional foods, regional specialties, and the greatest wine areas for tastings in our chapter on Croatian cuisine and wine, which will excite your taste buds.

In order to facilitate a hassle-free and pleasurable travel, we have compiled information on cultural norms, safety precautions, and practical tips into a separate chapter. Last but not least, we will present you with a conclusion that will emphasize the most important aspects of Croatia as well as provide you some further advice and suggestions that will encourage you to organize your own trip to Croatia.

Within the pages of this e-book, we have assembled a variety of resources, including recommended books and websites online, for more reading and investigation, which will enable you to delve even further into the enthralling world of Croatia.

Get ready to discover the hidden gems that Croatia has to offer, which range from its historic cities and untouched landscapes to its thriving culture and mouthwatering food. Allow Croatia Travel guides to be your reliable travel companion on this magnificent journey so that they can make certain that each and every one of your experiences in

Croatia is packed to the brim with awe and joy.

Chapter 1: Getting to Know Croatia

Croatia at a Glance: Geographical Overview

Knowing Croatia's physical layout can help you make the most of your time there. Slovenia, Hungary, Serbia, Bosnia & Herzegovina, and Montenegro are the countries that border Croatia in Southeast Europe. It has an impressive 1,246 islands, islets, and reefs spread out along its 1,100 kilometers of Adriatic Sea coastline. Croatia's varied landscapes, from the rugged Dinaric Alps to the lush Slavonian lowlands, make it an appealing destination for explorers of all stripes.

Croatia's Rich History and Cultural Heritage

Spend some time delving into the fascinating history of Croatia, which can be traced back to ancient times. The unique history of Croatia is reflected in the country's rich cultural legacy, which ranges from the Roman architecture of Split's breathtaking Diocletian's Palace to the enchanting Venetian architecture of Dubrovnik's Old Town. Explore Croatia's rich history through its many well-preserved UNESCO World Heritage Sites, which include castles from the Middle Ages, ancient ruins, and other historical sites. Discover the distinctive amalgamation of Croatian, Venetian, Ottoman, and Austro-Hungarian influences that have contributed to the formation of the character of the nation.

Climate and Best Time to Visit

The temperature of Croatia varies from area to region; thus, travelers may expect to encounter a wide range of conditions across the country. A delightful Mediterranean climate may be found along the Adriatic Coast, characterized by warm summers and somewhat moderate winters. The climate in inland regions is a combination of mountainous and continental, with winters being longer and colder and summers being longer and hotter. When you should go to Croatia relies heavily on personal choice as well as the kinds of activities you intend to partake in while there. The summer, from June through August, is the height of the tourist season, and during this time, coastal communities experience a surge in activity and vitality. Exploring towns and national parks is best done in the spring and fall, when temperatures are more moderate, there are less tourists, and sceneries are at their most beautiful. Those who are looking for a more peaceful experience will enjoy the winter months because skiing is an option in the hillier districts.

Festivals and Events in Croatia

The various festivals and events that are hosted all throughout the year in Croatia are what bring the country's thriving cultural scene to life. There is always something to excite and interest tourists, whether they come for the contemporary music and film festivals or the more traditional folklore festivals that celebrate the country's rich past. Feel the excitement of the Dubrovnik Summer Festival, which features performances of music, theater, and dance. The festival takes place against the breathtaking background of the city's old walls. Experience the spectacular spectacle of the Red Bull Air Race in Rovinj or get lost in the electric rhythms of Ultra Europe, one of the greatest electronic music festivals in Europe. These events provide a chance to enjoy the cultural richness that can be found in Croatia and to make memories that will last a lifetime.

You will be able to make the most of your time spent in Croatia if you have a firm grasp of the country's topography, if you are familiar with its illustrious past and cultural legacy, if you are aware of the most favorable time to travel there, and if you are conversant with its lively festivals and events. As you continue to read this book, we will offer you with further insights, practical suggestions, and recommendations that will assist you in navigating this fascinating nation with ease and ensuring that you build experiences that will last a lifetime.

Chapter 2: Essential Travel Planning

Visa Requirements and Travel Documents

It is imperative that you educate yourself with the visa requirements and travel papers that are necessary for admission into the nation before to going on your journey in Croatia. This should be done as early in the planning process as possible. Because Croatia is a part of the European Union, most tourists just need a passport that is still valid for the duration of their trip to be able to stay there for up to 90 days within a period of 180 days. However, in order to guarantee that you are in compliance with the relevant visa restrictions, it is vital to review the particular requirements that are dependent on your nationality. If you plan to remain for a longer period of time or have unusual travel restrictions, such as for business or academic reasons, it is recommended that you approach the Croatian Embassy or Consulate in your home country for additional information and help. They will be able to answer any questions you may have.

Currency, Banking, and Exchange Rates

The Croatian Kuna, abbreviated as HRK, is the country's recognized currency. Although some stores may take euros, it is best to have Kuna's on hand for day-to-day purchases because they are more common. The nation's airports, banks, exchange offices, and automated teller machines (ATMs) all offer currency exchange services to its customers. Get yourself acquainted with the current rates of exchange in order to guarantee that you are getting a good deal for your money. There is a widespread acceptance of major credit cards in tourist areas, hotels, and restaurants; nonetheless, it is always a good idea to have some cash on hand, particularly when traveling to smaller towns or patronizing enterprises that are locally owned.

Transportation Options: Getting Around Croatia

There are many different modes of transportation available in Croatia, making it convenient and easy to travel across the nation. Road travel is by far the most common, and there is a comprehensive system of highways and winding roads along the coast that are kept in excellent condition. When traveling to less populated locations or national parks, renting a car gives you the independence to go at your own leisure and explore the surrounding area. Alternately, Croatia is home to a sizable and well-developed public transportation infrastructure that links the country's major cities and towns with a network of buses and trains. The usage of buses as a mode of intercity transport is common since they provide an alternative that is both handy and cost-effective. For those interested in island hopping and discovering the Adriatic Coast, ferries and catamarans are accessible modes of transportation to link the major ports and islands. Walking or making use of other forms of local transportation, such as trams or taxis, are also viable options for traveling shorter distances within cities.

Accommodation Choices: From Budget to Luxury

There is a diverse selection of places to stay in Croatia that may be tailored to the preferences and budgets of individual tourists. A wide array of lodging options, ranging from those that are accommodating to travelers on a budget, such as hostels and guesthouses, to more upscale hotels and resorts, can be found around the country.

Beachfront resorts, quaint hotels, and cozy bed and breakfasts are just few of the types of hospitable establishments that may be found in abundance in coastal locations and other famous tourist sites. Hotels that are part of worldwide hotel chains as well as boutique hotels may be found in towns such as Zagreb. These hotels provide a variety of services and designs. Consider renting a classic stone home or apartment in one of the area's ancient villages or a private villa in the surrounding countryside for an experience that is more intimate and immersive. When searching for a place to stay, it is important to take into account a number of aspects, including its location, the facilities it provides, as well as customer evaluations. This will help you locate the ideal spot that is in line with your travel preferences and finances.

You'll be well-prepared to begin your tour across Croatia if you take care of the necessary paperwork for obtaining a visa, learn about the local currency and banking alternatives, investigate the various transit options, and choose the right place to stay. The enthralling locales, fascinating activities, and exhilarating excursions in nature that are awaiting your discovery in this wonderful nation will be introduced to you in greater detail in the coming chapters.

Chapter 3: Top Destinations in Croatia

Dubrovnik: The Pearl of the Adriatic

On the Adriatic coast, there is a city called Dubrovnik that is considered to be a real jewel due to its alluring beauty and extensive history. A trip to the Old Town of Dubrovnik, which is a UNESCO World Heritage Site, should definitely be on your itinerary. Traveling through its winding, limestone-paved alleys, which are lined with exquisite examples of medieval architecture, is like taking a step back in time. A breathtaking panoramic picture of the Old Town and the shimmering Adriatic Sea can be seen from the city walls and fortifications of the city. A trip to Lok rum Island, which is only a few minutes away by boat and is famous for its verdant gardens, historic ruins, and secluded coves, is the perfect way to get away from it all and relax.

Split: Ancient City with Modern Vibes

Ancient history and a thriving modern environment can both be found in Split, which is the second largest city in Croatia. The magnificent Diocletian's Palace, an astonishing Roman masterpiece that is located in the center of Split, is the city's most popular tourist attraction. Get disoriented in its maze-like alleyways, unearth mysterious plazas, and investigate historic temples and underground chambers. Hike up Marjan Hill, which is located in a beautiful park forest and provides a calm getaway, to get sweeping views of the city as well as the islands that are in the surrounding area. From Split, you can easily start on island hopping journeys to famous sites including as Hvar, Brac, and Vis, each of which offers distinctive landscapes, beach experiences, and cultural opportunities.

Zagreb: The Vibrant Capital

Zagreb, the capital city of Croatia, emanates a lively atmosphere that combines the allure of the ancient world with the buzz of the modern world. Begin your journey in the Upper Town (Gornji Grad), which is where you'll discover historical sites such as the St. Mark's Church with its colorful roof and the Zagreb Cathedral, which is a symbol of the city. Take a stroll around the Lower Town, also known as Donji Grad, where you'll find crowded squares, bustling marketplaces, and stylish stores. In addition, Zagreb is an important cultural center, as evidenced by the city's abundance of museums, galleries, and other cultural centers. Participate in the dynamic activities of the local art community, take in some live music events, or simply revel in the city's thriving café culture.

Plitvice Lakes National Park: Nature's Masterpiece

Plitvice National Park is a UNESCO World Heritage Site and one of the most outstanding natural treasures in Croatia. It is the perfect place to get away from it all and immerse yourself in the splendor of nature. Be amazed by the hypnotic flow of sixteen tiered lakes that are connected to one another by a seemingly endless number of waterfalls and are surrounded by verdant woodlands. You may take your time and explore the spectacular beauty of the park at your own speed thanks to the winding wooden footbridges and walking pathways. While hiking around the park, visitors have the opportunity to see a variety of animals, some of which are endangered, such as unique bird species. In the next chapter, you will learn some helpful information that will turn your trip to Plitvice Lakes National Park into an experience that you will never forget.

The travel experiences that can be had in each of these locations are really one-of-a-kind because of the distinct ways in which history, culture, and natural beauty are woven together. When you visit some of the most popular places in Croatia, you will come face to face with breathtaking natural scenery, architectural wonders, and a lively environment that will leave an indelible mark on you. In the next chapters, we will go further into each location, offering specific insights, recommendations, and information that is useful to enhance your trip there.

Old Town: UNESCO World Heritage Site

The UNESCO World Heritage Site that is the Old Town of Dubrovnik is like stepping into a time capsule as you stroll around it. Get disoriented in its winding labyrinthine alleyways, which are lined with spectacular examples of Gothic, Renaissance, and Baroque architecture. Be sure to take the time to appreciate the splendor of the Sponza Palace, the Onofre's Fountain, and the Church of St. Blaise, all of which are reminders of the glorious history of Dubrovnik.

City Walls and Fortresses

Begin an unforgettable adventure on the world-famous city walls that surround Dubrovnik. These historic defenses provide stunning vistas of the Adriatic Sea, the roofs of the city covered in red tiles, and the imposing Fort Lovrijenac. Walking along the city walls will give you a better understanding of the strategic importance that the city has always held throughout its lengthy history.

Lok rum Island and Nearby Attractions

Take the quick ferry voyage to Lok rum Island to get away from the hustle and bustle of the streets of Dubrovnik. This picture-perfect resort features verdant botanical gardens, secluded coves, and access to the glistening waters of the Dead Sea for those who like to go swimming. Do not pass up the opportunity to tour the picturesque mediaeval monastery and the fabled Iron Throne, both of which are located on Lok rum Island and are essential destinations for fans of Game of Thrones.

Diocletian's Palace: A Roman Marvel

Diocletian's Palace is a UNESCO World Heritage Site and is widely regarded as one of the Roman remains that has been kept in the best possible condition anywhere in the world. This enormous palace complex is home to a maze-like network of streets, retail outlets, dining establishments, and even residential neighborhoods. Within this live historical monument, you will be able to explore the peristyle, the underground halls, and the temple dedicated to Jupiter.

Marjan Hill and Park

Visit the tranquil sanctuary that is Marjan Hill to get away from the hustle and bustle of Split's city centre and to take in the beautiful views of the city and the Adriatic Sea. Explore the green park, go for a walk on its pathways or just have a picnic in the midst of the natural setting. At the same time that you may unwind and rest on Marjan Hill, you can take in the breathtaking scenery that Split's natural setting has to offer.

Nearby Islands: Hvar, Brac, and Vis

Your journey should continue beyond Split; cruise to the surrounding islands of Hvar, Brac, and Vis to continue your discovery. Hvar is well-known for its lively nightlife, beautiful beaches, and fields of lavender, whilst Brac is recognized for its world-famous Zlatni Rat beach and its picture-perfect coastal villages. Hidden coves, wineries, and a long and illustrious history all contribute to Vis's ability to provide a serene and genuine Mediterranean experience.

Upper Town (Gornji Grad) and Lower Town (Donji Grad)

Upper Town in Zagreb is a charming neighborhood that is located on a hill and is packed with historic landmarks, such as the mediaeval Stone Gate and Lotrak Tower. As you make your way down into the Lower Town, you'll come across lively squares, thriving marketplaces, and exquisite buildings that are home to museums, galleries, and other important cultural landmarks.

St. Mark's Church and Zagreb Cathedral

St. Mark's Church is noted for its unique roof, which is covered with the colorful coats of arms of Croatia, Dalmatia, and Slavonia. Admire the architectural marvels of this church while you are there. Pay a visit to the towering Zagreb Cathedral, a monument in the Gothic style that serves as a symbol of the city and provides an insight into the religious history of the region.

Museums, Galleries, and Cultural Hotspots

Visit the city's wide variety of museums, galleries, and other cultural attractions to fully immerse yourself in the booming cultural environment that Zagreb has to offer. Visit the Museum of Contemporary Art to learn about contemporary Croatian art, or head to the Croatian National History Museum to learn about the country's rich historical artefacts. The Museum of Broken Relationships provides visitors with an experience that is one of a kind and emotionally compelling.

Plitvice Lakes National Park: Nature's Masterpiece

Visit the awe-inspiring Plitvice Lakes National Park in order to get a true feel for the natural beauty that can be found across Croatia. Be amazed by the breathtaking sequence of lakes and waterfalls, all of which are encircled by verdant woodlands. Explore the park's system of wooden walkways and hiking paths, which will help you to get a better feel for this stunning UNESCO World Heritage Site.

The Stunning Cascade of Lakes and Waterfalls

The Plitvice Lakes National Park is well-known for its network of linked lakes and waterfalls, which together produce a breathtaking display of water falling from heights. Behold the hypnotizing colors of the lakes, which range from emerald green to azure blue as they merge together to produce an otherworldly panorama of natural beauty.

Hiking and Exploring the Park

Hiking excursions within the Plitvice Lakes National Park are sure to be among the most memorable of your life. Follow the well-maintained paths that are located throughout the park. These trails will take you through verdant forests, through breathtaking vistas, and along crystal clear lakes. Explore the area and look for tucked-away nooks and quiet places where you can sit back, take it all in, and marvel at the natural masterpiece that is before you.

Tips for a Memorable Visit

Consider the following helpful hints in order to get the most out of your time spent at Plitvice Lakes National Park. It is important to get there early to avoid the crowds, to wear shoes that are comfortable and appropriate for walking on rough terrain, and to bring along necessities like as water, food, and sunscreen. Accepting the laws and regulations of the park is one of the best ways to ensure that its natural state is maintained for future generations.

These best locations in Croatia provide visitors with a view into the country's illustrious history, breathtaking scenery, and lively culture. You'll make memories that will last a lifetime and get a greater appreciation for the natural splendor and cultural richness that Croatia has to offer if you take the time to visit these extraordinary places.

Chapter 4: Exploring the Adriatic Coast

The Adriatic Coast of Croatia is a magnificent region that provides visitors with a wide variety of activities and destinations to choose from, including picturesque beach towns and hidden jewels that are just waiting to be found. In this chapter, we will dig into the entrancing locations along the Adriatic Coast that will leave you enthralled, and we hope that you will join us on this journey.

Istria: The Tuscany of Croatia

Istria, which is located in Croatia, is frequently referred to as the "Tuscany of Croatia" because to its striking similarities to Tuscany, which is a well-known area in Italy. Istria, which can be found in the northwestern part of Croatia, is a region that has a rich cultural past and is characterized by its undulating hills, vineyards, and scenic villages.

Istria is widely regarded, much like Tuscany, for its breathtaking natural scenery. The landscape in this area is characterized by rolling hills that are blanketed in verdant vegetation, olive orchards, and vineyards that spread as far as the eye can see in every direction. A scene that is evocative of Tuscany is created by the beautiful magnificence of the area, which is peppered with mediaeval hilltop villages and typical stone buildings.

Istria is particularly well-known for its flourishing wine and food culture, which has been compared favorably to Tuscany's acclaimed culinary prowess. You may experience local kinds of wine, such as the renowned Malvasia and Teran, at any one of the region's plethora of wineries that are owned and operated by families. Visitors also get the opportunity to learn about the culture around truffles in the Istrian area, which is famous for the quality of its truffles. You may indulge in cuisines that use truffles, and you can even go on adventures that involve hunting for truffles.

The wine and truffles of Istria are just the beginning of the region's rich gastronomic heritage. The region is renowned for its farm-to-table philosophy, which features food that is both freshly prepared and sourced from the immediate area. You will be able to savour classic Istrian meals such as prosciutto from Istria (prut), traditional pasta from Istria (fui), seafood specialities, and exquisite olive oil.

Istria is home to a number of enticing seaside towns that ooze history and personality from every pore. The town of Rovinj, known for its winding lanes and brightly painted homes, is frequently compared to the Italian town of Portofino. The main city in Istria, Pula, is home to a Roman Amphitheatre that has been carefully conserved and is modelled after the Colosseum in Rome. These cities provide a vivacious spirit in addition to the stunning architecture and seaside promenades that they offer.

Istria also has a lot to offer those who enjoy exploring the great outdoors. Hiking, cycling, or just soaking in the stunning coastline vistas and pristine environment are all great ways to spend time in the region's national parks, such as Brijuni National Park and Cape Kamenjak, all of which include various landscapes and are home to national parks.

Istria and Tuscany have a number of similarities, not the least of which being their renowned scenery and gastronomic specialties. Both regions have a strong sense of tradition and a rich cultural legacy that includes historical landmarks, ancient ruins, and a long-standing history. Istria is characterized by a fusion of Roman, Venetian, and Austro-Hungarian influences, which may be seen in the region's architecture, cultural celebrations, and traditional practices.

Istria provides a mesmerizing experience that is reminiscent of the appeal of Tuscany. Whether you are interested in cultural discovery, food, nature, or simply a relaxed holiday, Istria has something to offer you. Istria has been referred to as the "Tuscany of Croatia" due to its rich gastronomic options, picturesque landscapes, and charming historical sites. This reputation is well deserved.

Pula and its Roman Heritage

In Pula, a city that is famous for its Roman ruins that have been carefully maintained, you may completely submerge yourself in the city's old Roman history. Visit the spectacular Pula Arena, an ancient Roman Amphitheatre that is being used today for a variety of events and performances. The interesting Archaeological Museum, the Temple of Augustus, and the Arch of the Sergei are all great places to see if you want to learn more about the Roman history of Pula.

Rovinj: A Charming Seaside Town

Rovinj is a charming beach town that is frequently referred to as the "Pearl of the Adriatic." Get lost in its twisting alleys and small streets, and be amazed by the pastel-colored houses that surround the shoreline. Climb to the top of St. Euphemia's Church for sweeping vistas of the town and the sparkling Adriatic Sea below.

Wine and Gastronomy in Istria

Istria is sometimes referred to as the Tuscany of Croatia, so be sure to treat yourself to the region's abundant culinary traditions. Visit some of the area vineyards to taste some of the world's best wines, which are made possible by the region's distinctive terrain and climate. Take pleasure in the tastes of classic Istrian meals that highlight the region's gourmet prowess, such as truffles, olive oil, fresh fish, and other traditional ingredients.

The Dalmatian Islands: A Sailing Paradise

The Dalmatian Islands, which are found off the coast of Croatia in the Adriatic Sea, are well known for their sailing opportunities.

They give a once-in-a-lifetime opportunity to go sailing thanks to the spectacular natural beauty of the area, the turquoise waters that are crystal clear, and the attractive coastal villages.

There are more than a thousand different islands, islets, and reefs that make up the Dalmatian Islands, and each one has a personality all its own. Hvar, Bra, Vis, Korula, olta, and Mljet are among the islands that sailors visit the most frequently. Other popular destinations include Mljet. These islands are well-known for the stunning scenery, quiet coves, and bustling harbors that can be found on them.

Sailing through the Dalmatian Islands is an excellent way to get to see a diverse range of locations within a very compact region. You may sail from one island to another, and along the route, you can come across some secluded beaches, some historic ruins, and some traditional fishing communities. Sailing from one island to another is made much simpler by the presence of several marinas and ferry services interspersed throughout the chain of islands.

In general, the weather conditions at sea in the Dalmatian Islands are favorable for sailing. Sailing conditions couldn't be better than those offered by the Adriatic Sea, especially during the warm summer months, when the winds are calm and consistent. The warm environment of the Mediterranean region offers comfortable temperatures and sunny weather, providing an ambiance that is favorable for activities that take place outside.

Sailing around the Dalmatian Islands affords visitors the chance to drop anchor in peaceful coves and investigate remote areas that are unreachable by foot or vehicle. This is one of the many attractions of the region. The seas are so clean that swimming, snorkelling, and diving are all enjoyable ways to explore the diverse marine life that lives below the surface of the ocean.

You'll discover enticing villages and communities with a rich cultural past all along the coast. Many sailing vacations begin at Split, a city known for its breathtaking Diocletian's Palace that serves as the port of departure. In addition to its reputation as the "Pearl of the Adriatic," Dubrovnik is home to a walled city that dates back to the Middle Ages and is a UNESCO World Heritage site.

An additional point of interest in the Dalmatian Islands is the regional food. In the seaside restaurants and pubs, you may feast on freshly caught seafood, olive oil and wines made in the area, as well as traditional Croatian meals. Sailors have access to a thriving nightlife and a variety of entertainment alternatives thanks to the islands, which play home to a number of summer festivals and events.

The Dalmatian Islands provide a variety of sailing opportunities suitable for sailors of all experience levels, making them an ideal destination for sailors of any background. In the event that you do not feel confidence in your ability to sail, you have the option of hiring a skipper or chartering a sailboat in order to traverse the seas. There are also yacht clubs and sailing schools that are available to provide instruction and rentals.

In conclusion, the breathtaking natural beauty of the Dalmatian Islands, favorable sailing conditions, abundant cultural legacy, and delectable food make these islands a genuine sailing paradise. Exploring these islands via boat gives you the opportunity to completely submerge yourself in the one-of-a-kind allure of the Adriatic coast and make memories that will last a lifetime.

Hvar: Lavender Fields and Nightlife

Hvar is a stylish island that is well renowned for its exciting nightlife, opulent resorts, and breathtaking lavender fields. Visit this island to experience its charm. Explore the alleys of Hvar Town, which date back to the mediaeval era, while strolling along the sophisticated promenade. Take some time to unwind on the island's picture-perfect beaches, explore the historic fortifications, and get lost in the buzzing atmosphere of the island's well-known nightlife scene.

Vis: Tranquility and Authentic Mediterranean Experience

Get away to the peaceful island of Vis, where you may experience nature in its natural state and the genuine allure of the Mediterranean. Visit the lovely town of Vis, which is characterized by its many stone homes and winding lanes. Discover secret coves, deserted beaches, and the entrancing Blue Cave, a natural wonder that glistens with brilliant shades of blue light.

Korcula: Marco Polo's Birthplace

Explore the island of Korcula, which is known for being the birthplace of the famous adventurer Marco Polo. Spend some time exploring the walled mediaeval town of Korcula, which is known for its winding lanes and spectacular architecture. Learn about the interesting life and travels of this famous explorer by paying a visit to the

Marco Polo Museum and reading about his experiences. Have fun exploring the island and taking advantage of its sandy beaches, wineries, and authentic food.

Zadar and Sibenik: Lesser-Known Gems

When contrasted to Croatia's more well-known tourist sites, the cities of Zadar and sibenik are hidden treasures on the Adriatic coast. These two cities each have their own set of distinctive attractions, as well as a more laid-back vibe.

The city of Zadar, which can be found in northern Dalmatia, has a long and illustrious past while nevertheless maintaining a buzzing, modern atmosphere. The historic district of the city is home to a wealth of architectural marvels, such as the Roman Forum, churches from the middle ages, and buildings constructed during the Venetian era. The Sea Organ in Zadar is a cutting-edge art work that is renowned for its ability to produce mesmerising musical sounds by utilising the movement of the waves. It is one of the most well-known attractions in the city. Visitors may also take in the breathtaking view of the setting sun from the neighbouring Greeting to the Sun, a big light work that is powered by solar energy.

The beautiful alleyways and tiny alleys of Zadar are packed with inviting cafes, high-quality restaurants, and quaint boutiques. It provides a setting that is more genuine and unpretentious, making it possible for tourists to totally submerge themselves in the culture of the area. The city is also known for its stunning beaches, which can be found both inside the city boundaries and on the islands that are close by, making it an ideal location for unwinding and basking in the sun.

sibenik is a mediaeval city that is well-known for the spectacular St. James' Cathedral, which is on the list of World Heritage Sites maintained by UNESCO. sibenik is located farther south along the coast. This outstanding example of Renaissance architecture is a must-see destination since it features beautiful stone carvings and a dome that is truly spectacular. The ancient town of sibenik is characterized by attractive squares, fascinating alleyways, and mediaeval walls; these elements combine to create an enchanting ambiance that is ideal for exploring.

Ibenik is also a gateway to the breathtaking Krka National Park, which is famous for its flowing waterfalls, crystal-clear pools, and lush foliage. sibenik is located in the central Dalmatia region of Croatia. The stunning natural scenery may be seen up close and personal by guests of the park on one of the guided boat trips or on one of the many hiking routes. Another hidden treasure that may be discovered through boat excursions is the adjacent Kornati Islands National Park, which is an archipelago that has more than one hundred islands and islets.

Each month of the year, the cities of Zadar and sibenik host a number of cultural events and festivals that honor the history, customs, and arts of the surrounding area. The vibrant atmosphere and genuine character of these cities may be experienced by tourists at a variety of events, ranging from music festivals to celebrations of local cuisine.

In comparison to other popular tourist locations, Zadar and sibenik provide a calmer atmosphere, less tourists, and the chance to explore lesser-known aspects of Croatian history and culture. This is one of the reasons why they are so popular. If you are interested in historical sites, natural beauty, or simply want to relax in a more tranquil setting, Zadar and sibenik are great alternatives for people seeking off-the-beaten-path experiences on the Adriatic coast of Croatia. Both of these cities are located on the island of Hvar, which is part of the Croatian Republic.

Zadar: Sea Organ and Sun Salutation

Explore the one-of-a-kind city of Zadar, known for its seamless integration of contemporary art pieces and historical sites. Be sure to take in the entrancing sights and sounds of the Sea Organ, an architectural wonder that composes beautiful music in response to the rhythms of the waves. Visit the Sun Salutation, a solar-powered installation that puts on a mesmerizing light show just before sunset and captivates tourists with its beauty.

Sibenik: Medieval Architecture and Krka National Park

Discover the mediaeval allure of Sibenik and its magnificent St. James Cathedral, an architectural masterpiece that is inscribed on the UNESCO World Heritage List and is embellished with ornate stone carvings. Visit the Krka National Park, a natural wonderland filled with waterfalls, cascades, and lakes of pristine clarity. Take a dip in one of the park's natural pools for a refreshing experience, and take in the jaw-dropping splendor of this unspoiled natural treasure.

Off-the-Beaten-Path Experiences

Explore the Adriatic Coast in search of undiscovered treasures and travel hotspots that are less well-known. If you want to find isolated beaches, lovely fishing villages, and uninhabited islands, you should take the route that is less travelled. Away from the madding masses, spend time interacting with the natives, savoring the local food, and embarking on one-of-a-kind excursions that will allow you to make cherished memories.

You will have the opportunity to take in the gorgeous landscape that Croatia's coastline has to offer if you go on an excursion along the Adriatic shoreline. This will be the case if you go on an excursion along the Adriatic seashore. Regardless of whether you are attracted to the Roman heritage of Pula, enchanted by the island appeal of Hvar, or drawn to the off-the-beaten-path adventures in Zadar and Sibenik, the Adriatic Coast provides a trip packed with amazing moments and boundless discoveries. This is true regardless of whether you are drawn to the Roman legacy of Pula, the island attraction of Hvar, or the off-the-beaten-path adventures in Zadar and Sibenik.

Chapter 5: Adventure and Outdoor Activities

Because of its varied topography and unspoiled natural surroundings, Croatia is a paradise for anyone who enjoy being outside and taking part in outdoor activities. In the next chapter, we will discuss the adrenaline activities that are waiting for you in the gorgeous outdoor playground that Croatia has to offer.

Kayaking and Sailing the Adriatic Sea

You are in for a treat if you decide to go kayaking or sailing around the Adriatic Sea; the seas are incredibly clear, and the coasts are really breathtaking. Paddle or sail your way through some of the most gorgeous bays, caves, and beaches in the area. Discover the beauty of the Elafiti Islands, which are close to Dubrovnik, the Kornati Islands National Park, and the Pakleni Islands, which are close to Hvar. Take in the soothing winds of the Adriatic, get up close and personal with a wide variety of sea life, and lose yourself in the peace and quiet of the water.

Hiking and Trekking in Croatia's National Parks

Put on your hiking boots and get ready for the adventures of a lifetime as you go across the national parks of Croatia. Explore Plitvice Lakes National Park and its magnificent sceneries by following the wooden walks that lead you through the park's flowing waterfalls and dense woods. Paklenica National Park is home to some of the most challenging hiking paths in the country, and they all provide stunning vistas of the surrounding cliffs and valleys. Visit the pristine wildness of Risnjak National Park and the awe-inspiring mountain peaks of Northern Velebit National Park. Both parks are located in Croatia. Every park in the system provides hikers and trekkers of varying skill levels with distinct options for hiking and trekking.

Scuba Diving and Snorkeling in Crystal Clear Waters

Explore the underwater world of the Adriatic Sea in Croatia, which is famous for its waters that are completely clean and the abundance of marine life that can be found there. Discover thriving coral reefs, caves hidden beneath the ocean, and shipwrecks dating back centuries. Explore the underwater wonders of the Kornati Islands, Vis Island, and the spectacular Bisevo Blue Cave, all of which are located close to Komiza. Whether you are a seasoned scuba diver or just starting out in the world of snorkeling, the clear coastal waters of Croatia are sure to provide you with experiences you will never forget.

Cycling Routes and Bike Tours

Get on two wheels and discover the picturesque scenery and quaint villages of Croatia by hopping on a bicycle. Cross the Istrian Peninsula on two wheels and enjoy the undulating vineyards, olive orchards, and lovely hilltop villages along the way. Dalmatia's coastline roads are truly something to behold, especially when viewed from a bicycle, thanks to the region's magnificent vistas of the Adriatic Sea. Follow the winding roads through the gorgeous scenery of the Dalmatian Islands, where you'll be rewarded with breathtaking views at every turn of the pedal. You may participate in organized bike tours or you can build your own adventure, exploring the countryside at your own leisure. Croatia is a great place to do either.

Nature lovers, those interested in experiencing new types of thrills, and people who enjoy being outdoors will find a diverse range of opportunities for adventure and outdoor activities in Croatia. Whether you prefer to paddle a kayak along the Adriatic Sea, trek through national parks, plunge into the depths of the sea or go on bicycle trips, the natural beauty of Croatia and the adventurous spirit of its people will leave you feeling thrilled and wanting more.

Chapter 6: Croatian Cuisine and Wine

The country of Croatia is not only a visual treat but also a delectable destination for foodies. In this chapter, we will dig into the mouthwatering world of Croatian cuisine and the rich wine traditions that make the country a paradise for people who are passionate about food and wine.

Traditional Dishes and Culinary Delights

Explore the myriad flavours and gastronomic delights that may be found in Croatian cuisine. Indulge in traditional meals such as Peka, which is a slow-cooked meat and vegetable dish made beneath a bell-shaped cover, or evapi, which is delectable grilled beef served with pita bread and a side of ajvar, which is a red pepper relish. Both of these dishes are prepared under a bell-shaped lid. Try some of the regional specialties made from seafood, such as risotto made with squid ink or fish that has been caught recently and cooked to perfection. Discover the diverse culinary traditions of each area, from the meals flavored with truffles found in Istria to the Mediterranean-influenced food found in Dalmatia.

Wine Regions and Tastings

Begin your immersion in the craft of winemaking with a trip that takes you through some of the most prestigious wine areas in Croatia. Take a trip to the Istrian peninsula, which is famous for the indigenous Malvazija white wine and Teran red wine. Discover the coast of Dalmatia and treat yourself to the strong reds and crisp whites of Plavac Mali and Poip, respectively. Explore the unexplored territory of Slavonia and find out why Graevina wines are considered the best in the world. Take part in wine tastings held in vineyards owned by families, gain knowledge about the many types of grapes, and savour the distinctive flavors and aromas that are characteristic of each wine area.

Local Food Experiences and Cooking Classes

Cooking lessons may help you hone your skills in the kitchen while also providing you with opportunities to learn about the regional cuisine. Participate in a truffle search in Istria and get the knowledge necessary to use these highly sought fungi in your cooking. Pay a visit to the local markets and strike up conversations with the merchants there while you shop for the fresh ingredients, you'll need to cook a typical Croatian dish. Master the technique of preparing pasta from scratch or bake some classic pastries like povitica or fritule. Take part in cheese-making workshops, olive oil tastings, or seafood cooking sessions, where seasoned chefs will walk you through the intricacies of Croatian cuisine and teach you how to prepare its signature dishes.

Traditional recipes, dishes influenced by the Mediterranean, and regional specialties all come together to form Croatia's unique culinary environment. Exploring the food of Croatia is a pleasant excursion into a world of flavours, scents, and cultural traditions, offering everything from farm-to-table experiences to immersive wine tastings. Whether you consider yourself a cuisine connoisseur or simply love indulging in regional specialties, the culinary scene in Croatia is sure to provide you with an experience you won't soon forget.

Chapter 7: Practical Tips and Cultural Etiquette

In this chapter, we will provide you with practical tips and valuable insights into

Croatian culture and etiquette. By familiarizing yourself with the local customs and knowing essential Croatian phrases, you can enhance your travel experience and navigate the country with ease.

Useful Croatian Phrases and Language Tips

It will be much easier to communicate with locals and make connections if you are familiar with important words and fundamentals of the Croatian language. Having a few key words at your disposal may make a world of difference, from simple exchanges of pleasantries and common expressions to the ordering of meals and asking for directions. To help you navigate discussions and build meaningful relationships with the people you meet on your travels in Croatia, we will present you with a helpful reference to key Croatian phrases as well as pronunciation suggestions.

Safety and Emergency Contacts

During your time spent travelling in Croatia, make safety a top priority by being acquainted with local safety rules and emergency contact information. We are going to go over several essential safety guidelines that you should keep in mind, such as being watchful of your personal items, utilising trustworthy transportation providers, and being generally cautious. In addition, we will provide you the necessary emergency contact information, which will include the phone numbers for the local authorities, an ambulance, and the tourist police. This will ensure that you are well-prepared for any unanticipated events that may occur.

Local Customs and Etiquette

Learn about the traditions of the local people and make an effort to behave in a manner that is befitting of the country of Croatia. Become familiar with the social customs, greetings, and actions that are typical in Croatia. It is important to familiarise yourself with local table manners, tipping practises, and clothing requirements to ensure that you respect the customs of the area while yet maintaining your sense of ease. Your ability to communicate well with people, cultivate good connections, and demonstrate a love for Croatian culture will all be enhanced by your knowledge of and participation in cultural etiquette.

By equipping yourself with useful Croatian phrases, prioritizing your safety, and respecting local customs, you will navigate Croatia with confidence and forge deeper connections with the people you encounter.

Embracing the cultural nuances of the country will not only enrich your travel experience but also demonstrate your respect for Croatian traditions and way of life.

Chapter 8: Resources and Further Reading

In this final chapter of "Croatia Travel Guides," we provide you with a curated list of resources and further reading materials to continue your exploration of Croatia even after you've finished reading this eBook. These resources will help you delve deeper into the country's history, culture, and hidden gems.

Recommended Books and Travel Guides

We highly suggest a variety of books and travel guides that do an excellent job of encapsulating the allure of Croatia so that you may broaden your knowledge and awareness of this fascinating country. These websites offer information on a wide variety of subjects, such as history, culture, food, and travel advice. This collection will direct you to useful materials that can improve your travel experience, whether you like narratives that are insightful and thought-provoking, guides that are both practical and informative, or photographic books that reflect the beauty of Croatia.

Online Resources and Websites

When it comes to organising a vacation to Croatia, the internet can be an invaluable source of information, and there are a variety of online tools and websites that may be of great assistance in this endeavour. We give a collection of reputable internet sources, travel websites, and official tourist portals that offer up-to-date information on a variety of topics relating to tourism, such as attractions, lodgings, and transportation. These tools can help you plan your schedule, find hidden treasures, and remain updated about any developments that are relevant to travel. These resources range from official government websites to travel blogs and forums.

Acknowledgments and Credits

The compilation of an exhaustive travel guide calls for the combined efforts and specialized knowledge of a large number of people. In this part, we would like to take the opportunity to thank all of those individuals who have assisted us in the production of this eBook. Their commitment and enthusiasm have been invaluable in bringing this trip guide to life, whether they were academics or travel writers, photographers or designers. In order to ensure that credit is given where it is due, we have made sure that throughout this eBook, we recognize the sources of information, photographs, and other materials that have been utilised.

Even after you've completed reading this guide, you may continue your voyage of discovery by reading the recommended books and travel guides, making use of the online resources and websites, and recognizing the efforts of those who have contributed to this guide. When you are planning your journey around Croatia, navigating its varied landscapes, and immersing yourself in the country's dynamic culture, the tools that we have compiled for you here will be invaluable companions and references.

We really hope that "Croatia Travel Guides" has supplied you with insightful knowledge, helpful hints, and invigorating ideas that will allow you to make the most of your time spent in Croatia. I hope that your travels are replete with life-changing moments, stunning vistas, and memories that you will remember forever. Have fun adventuring!

Conclusion

Congratulations! You have reached the conclusion of our in-depth guide to travelling around Croatia, a country known for its breathtaking natural scenery and many cultural traditions. As we get to the close of this eBook, let's take a time to review the most important information, provide some concluding advice and suggestions, and perhaps leave you feeling motivated to go on your own journey around Croatia.

Recap of Croatia's Highlights

In the course of this book, we have investigated some of the most alluring locations in Croatia, such as the Old Town of Dubrovnik, which is listed as a UNESCO World Heritage Site, and Plitvice Lakes National Park, which is an absolutely breathtaking location. We have explored the lively capital city of Zagreb, ancient monuments such as the Palace of Diocletian in Split, and the picturesque Adriatic Coast with its enticing islands. We have also explored the varied landscapes of Istria as well as the less well-known but no less beautiful cities of Zadar and Sibenik. After learning more about the history, culture, and cuisine of Croatia, we have a more profound appreciation for this unique nation.

Final Tips and Recommendations

As you get ready to go on an adventure in Croatia, here are some last-minute pointers and suggestions to help you get the most out of your time there. Check the prerequisites for obtaining a visa and ensure that all of your travel documents are in order. Get yourself acquainted with the local currency as well as the financial services and exchange rates before you leave. Make plans for how you will get about, whether you intend to go by own vehicle, public transit, or boat. Find a place to stay that fits your requirements, whether you're looking for something simple or opulent to get away from it all. Think about when you'd want to go depending on the weather and the festivals that will be going on, and don't forget to bring things like sunscreen, comfortable shoes, and a spirit of exploration with you when you go.

Inspiring Readers to Plan Their Croatian Adventure

The country of Croatia is home to a beguiling assortment of natural beauties, cultural treasures, mouthwatering food, and heartfelt hospitality. Every type of traveller may find a suitable activity in Croatia, whether they are interested in experiencing the local culture, venturing into the great outdoors, or simply relaxing by the aquamarine Adriatic Sea.

Permit the anecdotes and suggestions contained in this travel book to stoke your desire for adventure and encourage you to craft your very own adventures in Croatia that you will never forget. Your experience in Croatia is waiting for you to begin, whether it is seeing ancient sites and trekking through national parks, delighting in regional specialties, or making connections with the friendly people.

So, tell me, what exactly are you anticipating? Start making preparations for your trip to Croatia, often known as the Land of a Thousand Islands, and take advantage of the country's jaw-dropping scenery, thriving towns, and rich tapestry of activities just waiting to be discovered by you. Get ready to have your breath taken away by Croatia's stunning natural scenery, completely submerge yourself in the country's illustrious past and vibrant culture, and make new experiences that will stay with you for the rest of your life. Your journey across Croatia starts right here and right now!

Please Consider Writing an Amazon Review!

Are you enjoying this book? If so, please think about leaving a good review. It lets people know it's a good book and lets us
keep spreading our positive message. To review writing. Many thanks!

Printed in Great Britain
by Amazon